DISNEY THEATRICAL PRODUCTIONS
under the direction of
Peter Schneider and Thomas Schumacher
presents

AIDA

Music by
ELTON JOHN

Lyrics by
TIM RICE

Book by
LINDA WOOLVERTON
and
ROBERT FALLS & DAVID HENRY HWANG

SUGGESTED BY THE OPERA

Original Cast

HEATHER HEADLEY   ADAM PASCAL   SHERIE RENÉ SCOTT
JOHN HICKOK   DAMIAN PERKINS
TYREES ALLEN   DANIEL ORESKES

ROBERT M. ARMITAGE   TROY ALLAN BURGESS   FRANNE CALMA
CHRIS PAYNE DUPRÉ   THURSDAY FARRAR   KELLI FOURNIER   BOB GAYNOR
KISHA HOWARD   TIM HUNTER   YOUN KIM   KYRA LITTLE   KENYA UNIQUE MASSEY
CORINNE McFADDEN   PHINEAS NEWBORN III   JODY RIPPLINGER   RAYMOND RODRIGUEZ
ERIC SCIOTTO   TIMOTHY EDWARD SMITH   ENDALYN TAYLOR-SHELLMAN
SAMUEL N. THIAM   JERALD VINCENT   SCHELE WILLIAMS   NATALIA ZISA

Scenic & Costume Design
BOB CROWLEY

Lighting Design
NATASHA KATZ

Sound Design
STEVE C. KENNEDY

Hair Design
DAVID BRIAN BROWN

Makeup Design
NAOMI DONNE

Music Arrangements
GUY BABYLON
PAUL BOGAEV

Orchestrations
STEVE MARGOSHES
GUY BABYLON
PAUL BOGAEV

Dance Arrangements
BOB GUSTAFSON
JIM ABBOTT
GARY SELIGSON

Music Coordinator
MICHAEL KELLER

Technical Supervision
THEATRESMITH, INC.

Fight Director
RICK SORDELET

Casting
BERNARD TELSEY CASTING

Development Casting
JAY BINDER

Associate Producer
MARSHALL B. PURDY

Press Representative
BONEAU/BRYAN-BROWN

Production Stage Manager
CLIFFORD SCHWARTZ

Music Produced and Musical Direction by
PAUL BOGAEV

Choreography by
WAYNE CILENTO

Directed by
ROBERT FALLS

Originally developed at the Alliance Theatre Company in Atlanta, Georgia

ISBN 0-634-02964-9

Wonderland Music Company, Inc.

DISTRIBUTED BY

HAL•LEONARD®
CORPORATION

7777 W. BLUEMOUND RD. P.O. BOX 13819 MILWAUKEE, WI 53213

Contents

Sherie René Scott, Adam Pascal, Heather Headley

Heather Headley

EVERY STORY IS A LOVE STORY

Music by ELTON JOHN
Lyrics by TIM RICE

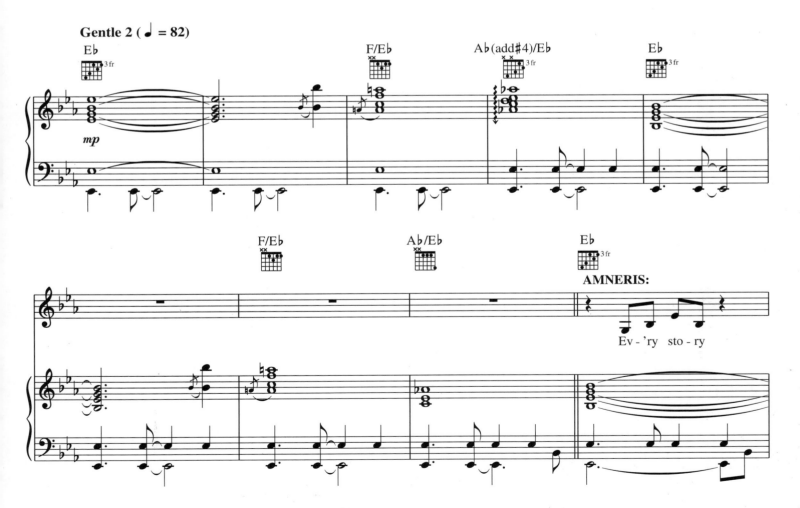

FORTUNE FAVORS THE BRAVE

Music by ELTON JOHN
Lyrics by TIM RICE

For - tune fa - vors __ the brave __

RADAMES:

We have swept to glo - ry, E-gypt's mas - ter - y _____ ex - pands __

From the Nile's __ north - ern del - ta to the dry, dry south-ern sands __ The

THE PAST IS ANOTHER LAND

Music by ELTON JOHN
Lyrics by TIM RICE

ANOTHER PYRAMID

Music by ELTON JOHN
Lyrics by TIM RICE

28

29

HOW I KNOW YOU

Music by ELTON JOHN
Lyrics by TIM RICE

MY STRONGEST SUIT

Music by ELTON JOHN
Lyrics by TIM RICE

ENCHANTMENT PASSING THROUGH

Music by ELTON JOHN
Lyrics by TIM RICE

Gently, not too slowly

To sail a-way__ to half dis-cov-ered plac-es__ To see the se-crets so few eyes__ have seen To see mo-ments of en-chant-ment on our fac-es__ The

RADAMES:

or understanding, from this humble palace slave.

But why did I tell her this? _ A strang - er I've just met A wom-an whom I hard-ly know at all ___ and will for - get ___ A-non-y - mous ___ and gone ___ to-mor - row _____

DANCE OF THE ROBE

Music by ELTON JOHN
Lyrics by TIM RICE

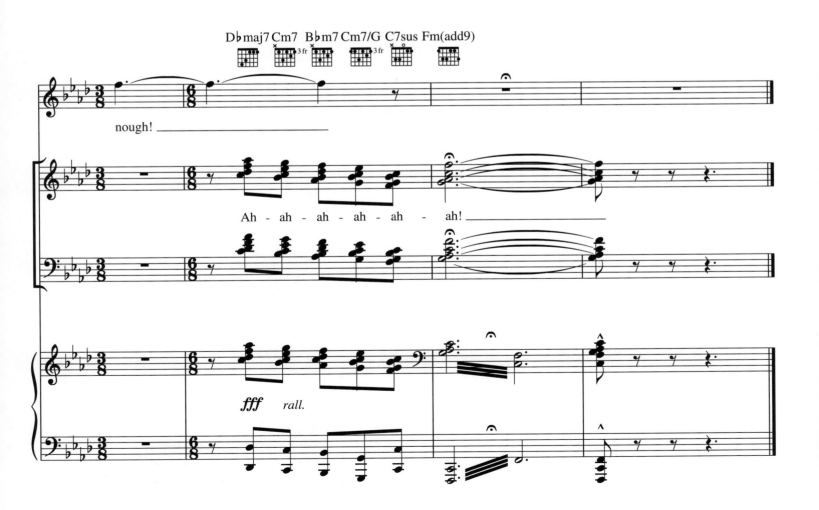

NOT ME

Music by ELTON JOHN
Lyrics by TIM RICE

With motion (feeling of 2)

AMNERIS:

(Spoken:) Why hasn't Radames come to see me again? We're to be married in three days, and yet, Aida, I must make

Repeat if needed   AIDA:

things right with him.

I shall not en - vy lov - ers __

But

long __ for what they share __

An emp-ty room is mer - ci - less __

AMNERIS:

Don't be sur - prised __ if I con - fess __

I need some com - fort there __

82

ELABORATE LIVES

Music by ELTON JOHN
Lyrics by TIM RICE

THE GODS LOVE NUBIA

Music by ELTON JOHN
Lyrics by TIM RICE

Measured, with inner strength

Take me in my dreams re-cur-ring Cheer-ful as a child-hood dance In-to

one more taste of free-dom One more long-ing back-ward glance In the

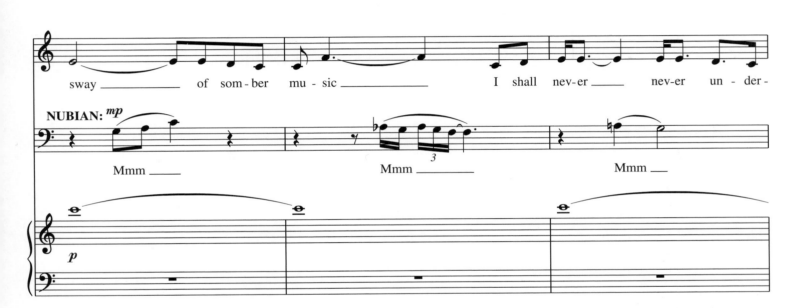

sway of som-ber mu-sic I shall nev-er nev-er un-der-

NUBIAN: Mmm Mmm Mmm

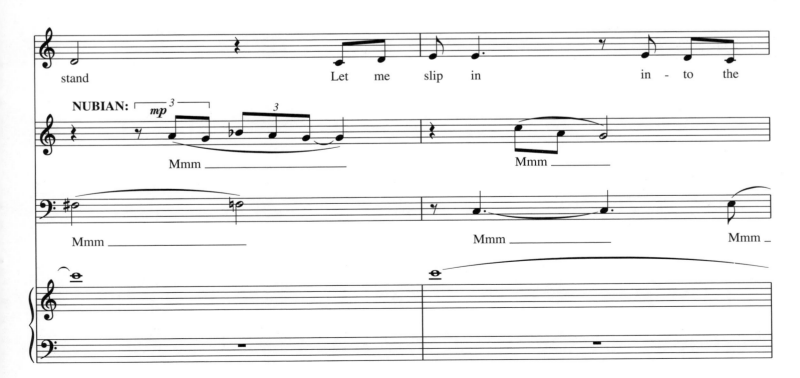

stand Let me slip in in-to the

NUBIAN: Mmm Mmm

Mmm Mmm Mmm

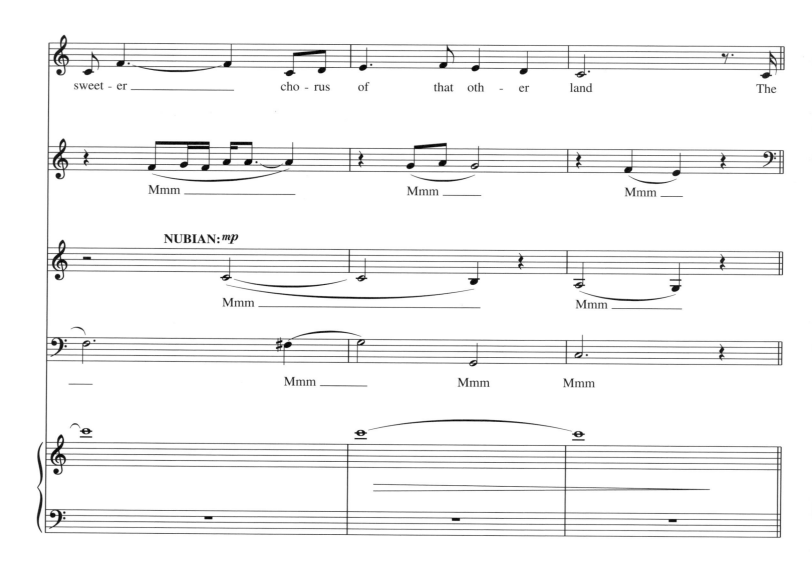

A STEP TOO FAR

Music by ELTON JOHN
Lyrics by TIM RICE

114

EASY AS LIFE

Music by ELTON JOHN
Lyrics by TIM RICE

LIKE FATHER, LIKE SON

Music by ELTON JOHN
Lyrics by TIM RICE

RADAMES' LETTER

Music by ELTON JOHN
Lyrics by TIM RICE

WRITTEN IN THE STARS

Music by ELTON JOHN
Lyrics by TIM RICE

I KNOW THE TRUTH

Music by ELTON JOHN
Lyrics by TIM RICE